Alcoholic Poetry

by Jasen P. Courtepatte

ISBN-13: 978-1530453504
ISBN-10: 153045350X

You can contact Jasen at: CallJToday@yahoo.ca
or connect with him on Instagram @AlcoholicPoetry

DEDICATION

This book is dedicated to my loving wife and my two beautiful daughters. Without your love and support, I would not be alive today.

JASEN'S STORY

As an alcoholic, perplexities surrounding the unexplainable and insane draw of alcohol will never cease to amaze me.

Chasing rock bottoms, looking for answers and always finding the same results.

A truly powerful addiction that takes many a life and leaves families in turmoil damaged beyond repair. My easy-to-read poetry will take you on a ride of the highs and dark lows of an alcoholic mind.

I am not a doctor and this book is in no way shape or form advice from a medical profession, but rather my own personal experiences with alcoholism.

The purpose of my book is to help you identify if you may or may not have a problem with drinking. If you or people you know can relate to my stories perhaps help is a consideration. I spent many years living in denial prior to admission of this disease. Many years... tormenting myself and my family because of the draw of the drink.

It's a very nasty sickness that became the most

important thing in the world to me. I couldn't sway my mind from the thought of alcohol to the point of near death.

With any luck, if you happen to share similar feelings towards the sauce, you may find solace in knowing recovery is possible. If a drunk like me can get sober so can anyone.

I have no idea what the future holds, but for today, I embrace sobriety and am so grateful for the copious benefits that accompany sober living. A drastic contrast from the dark days of a lost soul shackled to addiction.

Life wasn't heading in the right direction, alcohol promised so many things over the years.

Promised so much fun.

Promised so much relief.

Promised so much escape.

Promised it would be my "always there" friend….

Alcohol lied…

Difficult Times...

How did it happen,

when did it start?

Drinking took over,

and tore out my heart.

Chaos ensued,

the pull of the sauce.

All along thinking,

I was the boss.

A profound sadness,
head down in shame.
The draw of the bottle,
I can't seem to tame.
Powerful addiction,
controlling my world.
Head down in the toilet,
all while I hurled.
Handcuffs were cold,
tight on the wrist.
Had a firm grip,
but here is the twist.
Booze was the cuffs,
it kept me subdued,
Such a strong hold,
can't stop I'm screwed.

I promised never,

to ever drink again.

Booze lies were flying,

one turned to ten.

I drank...

not because

I had a problem

with alcohol.

I had a problem

with life.

The party was over,

hours in advance.

The booze in my system,

was taking a stance.

Started to drink,

early in the day.

Now no one wants me,

to come out and play.

Excuses, excuses,

I always got drunk.

Digging new holes,

the deeper I sunk.

I broke many promises,

to put down the drink.

The power of booze,

the deeper I'd sink.

I loved being drunk! Absolutely LOVED it, because I didn't know how to like being sober. I didn't start drinking at a young age like some people do. I waited until I was around 17, and even then, it wasn't very often. I was more interested in girls and sports, but whenever I did…it was always a runaway.

Coming home from a party, I was always the guy they'd have to pull the car over for…so I could throw up. I was the guy that would make a fool of myself at a house party.

I was the only one of my friends that had to go to the hospital to have an IV hooked up, because I drank too much. Always knew something was off.

Life is turbulent,

in an alcoholic mind.

Sometimes it's cruel,

and really not kind.

The only escape,

that there seems to be.

Is a drunk of all drunks,

a reality flee.

I don't like these thoughts,

of wanting a drink.

Knowing darn well,

the deeper I'd sink.

Life tests your limits,

unfortunately no joke.

Coffee and cream,

or a dark rum and coke.

Wine, beer, whiskey, rye,

all different poisons,

for this kinda guy.

I go to have one,

end up with ten.

And keep on repeating,

again and again.

Sneaking another,

drink from the stash.

Drunk once again,

a burnout and crash.

Hiding the booze,

not a very happy guy.

Living a life,

covering a lie.

Fallen soldiers,

on the ground.

Hidden bottles,

later found.

Drinking to

escape reality.

Reality is

I was an alcoholic.

Drink away pain,

drink to escape.

Drink 'til insane,

drink the green grape.

Not sure how to live,

life as it comes,

Happiness evades,

happiness runs.

A double rum and coke,

well that's a good start.

I'll have a few more,

I'm getting real smart.

Keep them coming,

get me some more.

Keep them coming,

'til I hit the floor.

Alcoholism told me

I didn't have the

Disease of alcoholism.

Alcoholism

is a

dirty liar.

Crying inside,

my screams are unheard.

Smile on my face,

but I don't say a word.

Addiction has crippled,

my spirit and soul.

The draw of the sauce,

has taken its toll.

Alcoholism is a progressive disease. It continues to grow in an alcoholic's lifetime, whether they drink or not. If I was to quit drinking today and pick it up 10 years down the road…I wouldn't pick up from where I left off, but rather where I would've been had I kept going.

It truly is a lifelong disease. I found this out the hard way…when after some longer term sobriety, I figured I had it under control. I figured…"one" glass of wine - no problem.

That "one"glass turned into an all out runaway, to the point of almost accidentally asphyxiating myself in my car. Had my family not found me, there's a good chance you wouldn't be reading these words.

Dealing with issues,

is a daily chore.

Drinking your problems,

will give you much more.

Covering up,

situations that arise.

Trying to drown,

loud internal cries.

When alcohol becomes

the most important

thing in the world.

You don't see the

glass or the ice –

just the next drink.

As a practicing alcoholic,

wanting to die.

Drinking and drunking,

with a tear in my eye.

Shattered reality,

wanting a grape.

Drinking and drunking,

all to escape.

Is it sweat,

or is it tears?

Dripping down,

my many beers.

Perhaps it knows,

the pain I'm in.

Perhaps it knows,

the pain it's been.

Romancing the drink,

like a long lost love.

The drink that was supposed,

to fit like a glove.

A life in despair,

a life in turmoil.

An addiction taking me,

back to the soil.

I stumbled, I fell,

ropes were getting tight.

Always a losing battle,

always a losing fight.

Drowning from drinking,

my emotional shape.

Drowning not swimming,

all for escape.

Whiskey, rum, vodka, gin,

beer and wine – let it all in.

Changing my vices,

had no effect.

Overboard with the saucing,

covering to protect.

Fears and anxiety,

jealousy and resentment.

That amongst others,

will hinder your contentment.

Stupid things I've done,

under the influence of rum.

Didn't make me smart,

rum made me dumb.

Woke up with bruises,

woke up with scars.

Surprised I didn't wake up,

locked behind bars.

How does it happen,

to get this way?

The pull of the sauce,

has got me at bay.

One is too many,

and twenty not enough.

Can't stop when started,

the fight is too tough.

Floating along,
on a big giant ball.
Drinking too much,
set for a fall.
Sailing through space,
fighting the drug.
Hopefully soon,
put the plug in the jug.
How much is too much,
and you've had enough pain?
You drink all your troubles,
but lose and no gain.
Chasing rock bottoms,
is taking a bite.
Losing a battle,
you don't need to fight.

Hockey trips, golf trips,

drinking with the boys.

Always going overboard,

took away the joys.

Dealing with triggers,

I'm angry, hungry, low.

I'm lonely, I'm tired,

I drink where I go.

Can't stop the drinking,

it's taking me down.

If there's a God up in Heaven,

have mercy on this clown.

Familiar habits,

leading you astray.

Robbing your happiness,

a devilish prey.

Wishing to stop,

but drink has a grip.

Trying to loosen,

the noose so to slip.

Head down in shame,

and full of regret.

My drinking has bought me,

a lost soul in debt.

Why can't I stop,

why can't I quit?

Help me God please,

help freedom fit.

Pouring rain,

inside my head,

Thunder clapping,

where's my bed?

Remorseful clouds,

full of haze.

Storm filled world,

drinking days.

Many have died,

trying to beat.

The addiction within,

that brought you defeat.

A powerful feeling,

you try to control.

With every passing day,

is taking its toll.

Sadly, I have seen this disease take lives. Over the past year of writing this book, I've seen three people buried.

One friend who went back to drinking three years ago, recently succumbed to liver failure. Two others took their own lives, because they just couldn't stop drinking.

It's a nasty disease that can sometimes end tragically in death. I have come to believe that while I'm staying sober…my disease is spending hours at the gym waiting for me to let my guard down.

Quite frankly, it's a fight I know I can't win if I ever start drinking again. I know for a fact that I have another "drunk" in me, but I don't believe I have another "sober" in me.

For today…I'm very grateful that I don't need to pick up a drink.

Stumbled and staggered,

tumbled and fell.

Falling down drunk,

and stink on my smell.

Drank too much,

drank too fast.

Holy freaking hell,

I hope it's my last.

Follow closely,

the trails of my tears.

Shedding loneliness,

shedding fears.

All of my emotions,

pent up inside.

Sometimes I want to,

run and just hide.

Alcoholism,

the family disease.

Affecting your loved ones,

your life it will seize.

Crushing your spirit,

and the ones you love most.

Your priorities, morals,

and soul it will roast.

Alcoholism is a family disease. It may be YOU taking the drink, but it is not only hurting you, it's hurting those around you. It's a very selfish, myopic behaviour that saddens loved ones.

Alcohol became the most important thing in the world to me. I would get defensive if anyone questioned my drinking. I would start to hide alcohol in and around the house. I became a professional, or so I thought, at sneaking drinks, however the only person I was fooling was myself. I would think about alcohol like the love of my life. Defending it. Holding it tight. Never leaving my mind. I would think of booze from the second I woke up to the second I put my head on the pillow at night. Planning out my next drink.

Numerous times over the years, I embarrassed my family because of my selfish desire for drink. I let them down and made it uncomfortable to be around me. I "vaguely" remember occasions where I said or did things that I never in a million years would have done sober. Looking back at some of those things now from a sober frame of mind, it still pains me that it happened, but I'm very grateful to have been forgiven for the mistakes of my ways. I'm very blessed that my family stuck around and supported me through the difficult times. I owe absolutely everything I have to finding sobriety and for that I'm eternally grateful.

Chasing rock bottoms,

I stand and then fall.

Can anyone hear me,

my cries when I call.

I need help,

and I want it real bad.

Constantly helpless,

hopelessly sad.

Many times in my life,

I've played the fool.

Drinking and drunking,

was my go-to tool.

Up to the day,

I came to a ridge.

I found myself tempted,

to jump off the bridge.

Patios are packed,

it goes with the season.

An excuse for a drink,

but I didn't need a reason.

Patio or not,

summer, spring or fall.

I'm an alcoholic,

I'm there 'til last call.

I was truly never installed a shut-off valve. I have never in my life understood the concept of having a drink or two. I mean…who the hell does that!

If you are going to drink...get drunk.

If I'm having one…I'm having 20 - Otherwise what's the point of empty calories?

And these people that are able to walk away leaving a half a glass of wine or beer…I don't understand!

That's like abandoning a soldier. You just don't do that.

But alas, I suppose that's why I have a problem. The old saying…"one is too many and 20 isn't enough" - is me in a nutshell.

Inappropriate behavior,

moral compass askew.

Barbed wire stomach,

pushing on through.

Doing all the things,

you know are all wrong.

An alcoholic mind,

thinks drink all along.

Stuck in the traffic,

of alcohol despair.

Can't stop the drinking,

life's seemingly unfair.

The turmoil is brewing,

at a very fast pace.

Blood pressure growing,

and heart seems to race.

Time to make a Change...

Decided to quit drinking,

now what's in store?

I'm scared of the future,

without the booze pour.

It is the correct decision,

I know in my heart.

Sick of being a drunk,

so now where to start?

Does it get better?

I really need to know.

This question I asked,

early in the flow.

How do you live?

Can you possibly survive?

Without drink in hand,

what keeps you alive?

Time to make some changes,

a scary time indeed.

God I need help,

addiction to be freed.

How to stop drinking,

put the plug in the jug.

If I don't seek outside help,

they'll bury my dead mug.

I drank for two and a half decades of my life. I always thought that I was maybe too old to quit. Having tried quitting numerous times with zero success, it wasn't until I hit bottom that sobriety found me.

If you happen to find yourself walking around a seniors lodge, try to find all of the hard core practicing alcoholics. No surprise – you won't! They passed away years earlier.

The human body is an amazing instrument, but wasn't designed to drink the way I was drinking and survive much longer. Put a plant in a vase of alcohol and see how it reacts. My insides were crying for help and I wasn't listening to the screams.

The time has finally come,

to make a big life change.

Choices to be made,

a life to rearrange.

"When" is finally here,

I've been fighting for so long.

If I don't quit drinking,

I'll sing the same song.

You're never too old,

to make a life change.

I was well in my 40's,

making a life rearrange.

Close to my death,

walking thin lines.

Glad I was able,

to read all the signs.

A very vague way,

to look at recovery,

It's a nice little journey,

a journey of discovery.

Finding health,

and cleaning the street.

Maintaining it all,

and the ones that you meet.

Lost in the forest,

lost in the trees.

The draw of the sauce,

is too much for me.

Sound familiar,

to you - drinking friend?

Not to worry,

you're soon on the mend.

Becoming an alcoholic,

was not top of my list.

Recognizing I was one,

gave me serenity I'd have missed.

Alcoholic, or not,

battling strife.

Sober way of living,

is a great way of life.

One really good way,

to battle addiction,

Is to listen to others,

with the exact same affliction.

Sharing and hearing,

inspiration and hope.

Might be what you need,

to get off of the rope.

Wherever I went,

I assumed all were drunk.

As it turned out,

I was a solo drunk skunk.

Easy to assume,

all were like me.

When I got sober,

it was plain to see.

Christmas time was always a good time. Office parties, restaurant lounges packed, people celebrating. It was always a good time to blend in with the drinking. But come the new year, everyone else stopped...and I kept going.

When I sobered up, I realized that not everyone had been drunk like me. My disease had told me they were. It's much like the golf tournaments that I entered.

I always assumed everyone else around was drunk, as they often supplied free drinks. Once getting sober, I realized how wrong I was. It was usually just me that had been drunk.

Figure out the

root of your problems,

before your problem

lays below the roots.

I see people on a daily

basis...

Show me their strengths,

by letting go of their

weaknesses.

Unfortunate rock bottom,

is sometimes a grave.

The draw of the poison,

you have to be brave.

To step outside,

of a comfortable place.

To reach out for help,

and give your soul grace.

Some people struggle,

I've been there before.

Life time of challenges,

but you don't need the pour.

The turn back to addiction,

ends in one of two ways.

You learn how to like sober,

or where the worm plays.

Visiting alcoholism,

days of the past.

Had I not exited,

my life would not last.

A tumultuous place,

to stop in for a while.

A whole lot of sorrow,

with nary a smile.

I resemble an alcoholic,

people say not.

When I ask what that is,

brown paper bag they are
taught.

Let me help you out,

walking amongst you we do.

Every demographic,

if only you knew.

I'm 100% certain,

that 100% of the time.

I had drinking under control,

0% of the time.

Common misconception,

rainbows and candy.

When you get sober,

immediately dandy.

Fact of the matter,

everything is vivid.

The carnage of the past,

can make you a bit livid.

Don't let fear,
stop you from living.
Use it to thrust you,
into a world that is giving.
Share your story,
give what you can.
Tell your struggles,
stick to the plan.
Help others out,
lift when they fall.
Enrich others lives,

keep standing tall.

To an alcoholic like me,

what's the cost of a beer?

Not $5 or $6,

like it is for a peer.

To me it's a house,

a wife and a car.

And that's if I'm lucky,

and don't take it that far.

Fear is a powerful emotion that makes my mind think crazy things. I've heard that fear is False Evidence Appearing Real.

For me, I can take the smallest of little things today, and forecast down the road making these small issues the biggest of life altering events. Nine times out of 10, nothing ever happens. And even if it does, it works out much better than I ever could have expected.

Leading up to these non-existent events, I really didn't enjoy life like I could have. When realizing that fear was only existing in my head…it made living that much better.

Fear is born, raised and lives between your ears.

Trying to find flaws,

in others we know.

Is a sign of our own,

insecurities in tow.

As I look back,

am I happy, am I sad?

I can say with certainty,

experiences I've had.

Drinking days gone,

just for today.

To plan for the future,

could cause me to stray.

Hump day happy,

hangover free.

Happiness happens,

hang on and see.

Leaving all the wobbles,

the fall downs behind.

Heaving all the hangovers,

happiness you find.

How many more,

excuses can you make.

For boozing and drunking,

and drinks that you take?

Wish I could quit,

but I can't so keep going.

Whatever your excuse,

it's your life you are blowing.

Another Saturday night,

sober dude I will be.

If you want a few drinks,

you're safe driving with me.

One less drunk,

out on the road.

Thoroughly grateful,

in sobriety mode.

Life is good,

no drink in my hand.

Sober and happy,

and grateful I stand.

The freedom that comes,

from plugging the jug,

brightens the smile,

on my once crying mug.

The loss of my dog,

one week ago,

has taken its toll,

like some never know.

A profound sadness,

after losing a pet,

but don't need the booze,

as my safety net.

Living my life,

as life moves along.

Sobriety is critical,

a drink would be wrong.

Battling alcoholism,

on your own 'til you fall.

Is much like nailing,

a custard pie to a wall.

It's a futile struggle,

with limited results.

Because we are human,

with character faults.

Alcoholic paths,

previously trod.

Like running your toes,

through freshly laid sod.

A comforting thought,

a glimmer of hope.

That you too can get sober,

no matter the scope.

Maintaining sobriety,

is a daily chore.

A life that is better,

than ever before.

Hard to imagine,

when caught in disease.

That a life could be better,

once brought to my knees.

I was speaking at a college one time. A lady in the crowd asked a question. She said where she's from, if you got drunk, had a drink, or even posted a picture online holding a glass of wine… you would be deemed an alcoholic and it was frowned upon. She asked "how does society treat you as an alcoholic"?

I said look around. There is a liquor store on every corner here. Alcohol is glorified and sexified. When I was younger, 'happy hour' used to be on Fridays at 3:00 or 4:00. Now it's everyday and in some establishments everyday all day.

It has become such a common accepted fixture in society these days. It's promoted as fun and a way to escape. For a problem drinker like myself however, all it does is add more problems to my already problem-filled plate. So to answer her question,..I'm very well accepted in society. I'm a proud non practicing alcoholic. I always will be an alcoholic. And I'm good with that.

Accepting that fact was the first step to recovery. In fact opening up to my disease has opened the floodgates to others coming forward asking for help. My 'Happy Hour', never truly began until I quit drinking.

You're only as sick,
as your secrets you keep.
A turmoil of feelings,
in the gut buried deep.
Relieving yourself,
of a worried troubled past.
Get rid of addiction,
make sobriety last.
Triggers come,
and triggers go.
Simple thoughts,
let 'em flow.
Laugh it off,
dismiss 'em all.
Move along,

standing tall.

Using alcohol,

to dull the pain.

Abusing addiction,

is clearly insane.

I know what it does,

I've been there before.

Not interested in visiting,

the pain anymore.

I live in a city,

a liquor store every mile.

I keep on driving,

with a big smile.

A definite contrast,

from days of old,

when I'd fall down drunk,

or so I'm told.

How could you possibly,

have fun without drinking?

It's Friday again,

happy hour I'm thinking.

Happiness for me,

truly only started,

when I put down the drink,

and we gladly were parted.

I've got no booze in my system,

and that is ok...

My name is "J" and

I like it that way...

Life is good today.

Life is good today.

So grateful to be sober,

but have to be cautious.

The disease always there,

that once made me nauseous.

Now in the past,

at least for this day.

One day at a time,

and sober I'll stay.

Glass full of booze,

promised so much.

Now nothing further,

would I wish to touch.

Alcohol depleted,

and robbed me of peace.

Sober and happy,

I've got a new lease.

Always help available,
if you suffered like me.
A willingness to stop,
and a hope to be free.
Too much pain,
you're carrying inside.
The drink is the symptom,
you're using to hide.
Happy and clean,
and free of the shackles.
Handcuffs are off,
but addiction it cackles.
Always there,
sitting in wait.
But I have the tools now,
to control my own fate.

Saturday night,

out on the town.

No longer drunk,

no longer the clown.

What I once thought,

was fun with the sauce,

never turned out being,

as booze was the boss.

Golfing with my buds,

bevy cart always near.

Never ever a bad time,

when chugging the beer.

At least that's what I thought,

if I could stop at just a few,

but that would never happen,

and everybody knew.

I used to golf as an excuse to drink for six or more hours at a time. It was funny - if I was going golfing and you were to say to me "HERE have a dozen orange juices or a dozen chocolate milks or even a dozen waters," I'd say…you're crazy! Who's drinking a dozen of any of those things?

If you were to say "Here is a dozen beer," I would say…"That's a good start to the front nine! What are we drinking for the back nine?"

Now in sobriety, being on a golf course is an amazing life pleasure. I truly appreciate the sport and being in nature versus escaping life like I once did. Plus…my game has improved immensely.

Mornings are better,

not carrying the thought.

Of a night of disaster,

and forgiveness to be sought.

No hangovers today,

and feeling serene.

Glad to be sober,

on the golf green.

Life can be mean,

life can be cruel.

Drinking your problems,

you may be the fool.

Drinking doesn't remove them,

or make them disappear.

Drinking exaggerates them,

and gives you more fear.

We all have life issues,

seemingly unresolved.

Driving while drinking,

none of them solve.

Taking your ignorance,

out behind the wheel.

Is a very selfish act,

as lives you do steal.

Sunday afternoons,

used to be TV and drink.

Drowning in sorrows,

and deeper I'd sink.

Health is the choice,

I choose on this day.

Gives me the chance,

to live life and play.

No room for ego,
when battling the disease.
Let go of pride,
and give it some ease.
We get in our heads,
and want the control.
When that is what hurts us,
and crushes our soul.
I had someone ask...
Why not just have one?
I'm deathly allergic,
and I'd be no fun.
If I could cut it,
to one or just two,
I'd be a normal drinker,

and not have 52.

Over-think the problem,

will cause too much worry.

Twist and turn your mindset,

will make your day dreary.

The bad of what you build up,

never seems to play.

Made up situations,

in your head they stay.

We are here to live life,

to achieve and succeed.

Some turn to addiction,

and falter indeed.

Addiction takes a toll,

on family and friends.

Learning to cope,

navigates bends.

Sleeping is easier,

with a head free of worry.

Alcohol troubles,

make minds very blurry.

Peaceful good nights,

and nights full of rest.

Are definite perks,

of the weight off your chest.

Start of the season,

for a golfer like me,

the 19th hole,

I surely would be.

Falling down drunk,

after a day of boozing.

Now sober days,

is what I am choosing.

Morning sunshine...
from a sober mind.
A glorious place,
like no other kind.
The days are better,
the days are brighter.
When you finally clean up,
experience from this writer.
Patio chairs,
and long summer days.
Warmth of the sun,
and drinks in the shade.
'Tis the season,
to be outside.
You don't need booze,

to enjoy the ride.

Baileys and coffee,

a good start in the past.

Good so I thought,

but the good did not last.

Today is a bit different,

coffee and cream.

Shut down the nightmare,

turn on the dream.

Life is going to challenge you,

and give you some tests.

Like the loss of a career,

or loss of our pets.

A drinker's mind overplays,

all of the strife.

Deep breaths my friend,

it's still a good life.

Congratulations!

You awoke from your rest.

You're winning at life.

You're passing the test.

Life is fighting for

your sobriety.

Life is just asking you to

join the battle.

Holding resentments,

is bringing you down.

Clutching the past,

is life's ugly frown.

Drop the resentments,

release the pain.

You owe it to yourself,

to be happy again.

In the movie of

Alcoholism...

I did my own stunts.

In the follow up movie of

Sobriety...

I play the role of passenger.

Alcoholism beat enough

out of me to leave

just enough space for

sobriety to blossom.

Voices dance,

between your ears.

A ballet of objections,

and anger and fears.

Taking a toll,

if you let it get away.

Settle the voices,

get on with your day.

In sobriety...

admitting defeat,

is winning the fight.

So many people,

affected by the drink.

So many times,

pushed to the brink.

Time to surrender,

time to give in.

Time to give up,

time to win.

Your path leads to

wonderful places.

Make sure nobody else is

forging your trail.

We all have scars,

some visible some not.

Beautiful indications,

of a fight that we've fought.

Delicate imperfections,

of a wonderful existence.

Dealing with life,

with a growing persistence.

We're under the same moon,

both me and you.

We meet for a reason,

I know this to be true.

It's not just a concidence,

that my words you are reading.

We are helping each other,

and our souls we are feeding.

We all know an alcoholic,

some of us look in the mirror.

What plays between your ears,

is what you should fear.

How we all handle,

the situations we face.

Will help you handle life,

without utter disgrace.

Walking through life,

it's easy to forget.

To stop and smell the roses,

think of the people you've met.

While deep in addiction,

there are things that you miss.

When sobering up,

it's life that you kiss.

The people that make you smile,

hold on to them tight.

Get rid of the ones,

who only want to fight.

Life is too short,

to not be respected.

Hold good friends close,

make them feel like they're selected.

You're not alone,

in your struggle with addiction.

Give the disease,

the notice of eviction.

I love seeing people get well and succeed in sobriety! I've fought this disease for far too long. It impacted many lives around me and I know the pain associated with it all too well.

If you go to a boxing match and a fighter throws in the towel...they lose the fight. The exact opposite awaits you with sobriety. In sobriety, when you throw in the towel to the beating of the drink....you win the battle!

Fighting a hopeless, painful fight can lead you to your grave. Perhaps it's time to get your life back! Throw in the towel! Join the winning team!

You want it...and I want it for you!

I know both sides of the track my friend, and I can tell you unequivocally that the sober side is a much, much better way to navigate life.

Hopefully these pages will help you to identify what you may have known all along. If you can relate to any part of my book....perhaps you may have a problem with drinking.

About the Author

Jasen Courtepatte is a respected professional in society, loving husband and father of two and is a recovering alcoholic. Battling addiction for many years as a functioning alcoholic, Jasen lived a life where he loved being drunk, because he did not know how to like being sober. Although he wanted desperately to quit drinking, it seemed he continued to chase rock bottoms.

His final rock bottom, which by the grace of God was not death, resulted in him seeking the help that is out there and truly committing to it. Jasen now speaks at various venues such as hospitals, recovery centres, detox facilities and colleges.

He meets so many people from various demographics suffering from the same disease. One of the common questions asked is "am I an alcoholic?"

Jasen has written this book with the idea that if you can relate to any of the pages…*perhaps* you may have a problem. Jasen is dedicating his life to helping other alcoholics, as he knows first hand the struggles and pains associated with this very painful disease. It does kill, but there is hope. Jasen is also a monthly contributor to an online recovery magazine.

You can contact Jasen at: CallJToday@yahoo.ca
or connect with him on Instagram @AlcoholicPoetry

$$\begin{array}{r} 1 \\ 28 \\ \times\ 2 \\ \hline 56 \end{array}$$

$$\begin{array}{r} 1 \\ 39 \\ 2 \\ \hline 78 \end{array}$$

$$\begin{array}{r} 39 \\ 2\overline{)78} \\ 6\ \downarrow \\ \hline 18 \end{array}$$

42517101R00081

Made in the USA
San Bernardino, CA
05 December 2016